ALL DAY RECIPES

Think A Complete Meal

A. K. Hayes

ISBN: 9781693150371

DISCLAIMER

We have used our best efforts in preparing the Think a complete meal Book, and the information is provided "as is." We make no representation or warranties with respect to the accuracy or completeness of the contents of the cookbook and we specifically disclaim any implied warranties of merchantability or fitness for any particular purpose.

All material in the Think a complete meal Book is provided for your information only and may not be construed as medical advice or instruction. No action or inaction should be taken based solely on the contents of this information; instead, readers should consult appropriate health professionals on any matter relating to their health and well-being.

WE DO NOT CLAIM TO BE DOCTORS, NUTRITIONISTS OR DIETITIANS. THE INFORMATION IN THE THINK A COMPLETE MEAL BOOK DOES IS MERELY OUR PERSONAL OPINION AND DOES NOT REPLACE PROFESSIONAL MEDICAL OR NUTRITIONAL ADVISE.

TO MY READERS

As an author, my books are useless if I don't have anyone to read them. I believe I have a great community of readers because I enjoy all the dramas that you are all giving me. All your positive and negative comments are all appreciated.

I want to use this medium to thank all my readers for always reading my books. You are all awesome. You are the reason I feel like writing on new topics every day.

I do read all your comments on my page and all the reviews. Keep pumping in the reviews. They are very important to me because they make me fix errors in my writing.

I am grateful.

Love from…

A. K. Hayes

ABOUT BOOK

This book contains vital information about complete breakfast, lunch and dinner Recipes.

This book conveys many and unlimited benefits, which can guarantee you living a healthy life forever. The complete Diet is a nourishing diet which appears to benefit most people.

This book will reveal the benefits of a complete diet to you that will enable you live and enjoy a healthy and blissful life.

TABLE OF CONTENTS

DISCLAIMER   iii

TO MY READERS   iv

ABOUT BOOK   v

TABLE OF CONTENTS   vi

INTRODUCTION   x

BREAKFAST MEALS   1

    MILLET MUFFINS   1

    BASIC BREAD   3

    BASIC SWEET BREAD   5

    ALMOND BUTTER COOKIES   7

    BETTY CROCKER BROWNIES   9

    BUTTERMILK BISCUITS   11

    CARROT DROP COOKIES   13

    CHOCOLATE CHEW   15

    DATE-NUT SCONES COOKIE   16

    FARINA COOKIES   18

    GRAHAM CRACKERS   20

    CHEESE HAM CASSEROLE   22

    CHEESY RICE RAMEKINS   24

    CHUNKY CHEESE BREAD   26

AVOCADO ANGEL EGGS   28

BREAKFAST CASSEROLE A BAKED EGG, SAUSAGE, &
BREAD CASSEROLE   30

BREAKFAST CASSEROLE   32

HAM CASSEROLE   34

BREAKFAST SAUSAGE CASSEROLE   36

BREAKFAST TORTILLA STRATA   38

LUNCH MEALS   **40**

APPLE BEEF CHILI   40

BASIC BEAN BURGERS   42

BEAN & RICE BURGERS   44

BEAN CASSEROLE   46

BEAN CURD ROLLS   48

BEAN CURRY   50

BEAN PATTIES   52

CHILI NACHOS   56

CREOLE BEAN PATTIES   58

3 SOUP CROCKPOT ROASTS   60

A DIFFERENT CHICKEN NOODLE SOUP   62

ACORN SQUASH SOUP   64

ALASKAN CLAM CHOWDER   66

BARLEY STEW   68

BEER & CHEESE SOUP   70

CALICO BEAN SOUP   72

CHICKEN TAGINE   74

EASY CHILI   76

FISH STEW   78

DINNER MEALS   **80**

ALL DAY MACARONI & CHEESE   80

APPLE MINT COUSCOUS (SAUCE FOR LAMB)   82

ASPARAGUS PASTA   84

BRIGHTON BEACH BAKE   86

SPINACH PASTA   88

ALMOND TOPPED PEAR PIE   90

AMISH PEACH PIE   92

BLACKBERRY PIE   94

CHEESE CUSTARD PIE   96

CRANBERRY PEAR PIE   97

ACINI DI PEPE SALAD   99

BLACK BEAN & BARLEY SALAD   101

BLACK EYED PEA SALAD   103

CHERRY DELIGHT SALAD   105

CHINESE CHICKEN SALAD   106

CONGEALED SALAD   108

APPLE HARVEST OATMEAL   109

BATTER CRISP ONION RINGS   110

BORANI ESFANAA	112
CAULIFLOWER CHERRY LONGHORN	114
CREAMY PARSNIP MASH	116
EGGPLANT/SWISS CHEESE CASSEROLE	118
THINK A COMPLETE MEAL	**120**
FROM THE AUTHOR	**122**

INTRODUCTION

This may be very basic and elementary, but having different food groups with a meal will make it much more effective in several ways. By doing this, you can get more out of your meal such as more energy later on, have more variety and tastes in your meal, and generally enjoy your meal more because of this.

I've seen several people who will just have one type of food as their entire meal, and that really doesn't make for a very fulfilling, nutritious, or exciting meal. An excellent example of this would be a single entrée TV dinner. We've all seen them in the frozen foods section in grocery stores. Whether it's just a serving of rice with broccoli and cheese, turkey and gravy, or Salisbury steak, it's not a complete meal. Of course, we buy them for convenience, but they don't really provide us with a very fulfilling meal. They are usually high in fat and preservatives, and they usually are just what they say: an entrée, nothing more. Not to mention, these entrées don't really provide us with a lot of nutritional value as well. I'm not saying that eating TV dinners should be avoided completely, but perhaps eating a cooked vegetable or salad to go along with the entrée would be very beneficial nutritionally, and in the long run, keep you full longer, and your body will get much more efficient use out of the meal. In my opinion, an entrée should never take the place of a complete meal. Whether you're cooking at home or eating out, balancing your meals is very important. When I lived at home when I was younger, my father would always just make himself a grilled cheese sandwich if my mother was not home for some reason to cook for all of us. Not that my father didn't know how to cook, he simply didn't want to invest the time and energy into making a more complete meal. I would usually get on his case about it telling him that a grilled cheese sandwich isn't a meal by itself.

By balancing your meals with different food groups, your body will be able to digest the meal more efficiently, giving you more energy and benefits from the meal. This can help your overall mood, energy level, general health, and help your body function better in many ways. This can also help with intestinal aches and pains or problems, such as constipation, can also be minimized by following these simple guidelines. I guess my advice is the next time you want a meal for convenience or simply don't want to invest the time into cooking a complete meal, remember that in the long run you'll be a lot more satisfied in many ways if you provide yourself an entire, balanced meal.

BREAKFAST MEALS

MILLET MUFFINS
CATEGORIES: BREAD, MILLET

Ingredients:
1 1/2 cup Millet flour

1/4 tsp Orange flavoring
1/2 Cup Soy flour
1 Cup Water/orange juice
1 tbsp. Baking powder
1/2 tsp salt optional
1/4 Cup Vegetable oil
1/4 Cup Rice syrup/honey

Instructions:
Combine all dry ingredients in a medium bowl. Mix all liquid ingredients then add to dry ingredients. Put the mixture in a well-oiled muffin tin. For bread Bake at 375F for 15--20 min 35--40 for loaf/till done.

Prep time: 30 min   **Cook time:** 50 min
Nutritional Info: Calories: 176 | Total Fat: 7.7g | Cholesterol: 12mg | Sodium: 268mg | Potassium: 109mg | Total Carbohydrates: 24.8g | Dietary Fiber: 2.4g | Protein: 3.7g | Sugars: 10g

BASIC BREAD
CATEGORIES: BREAD, SUGAR, YEAST, EGG, MAKE 2 LOAVES

Ingredients:
1/4 cup sugar
3 tbsp. shortening
1 tsp salt
3/4 cup 2% milk
1 packet yeast
1/4 cup warm water
1 egg
3 1/2 cup flour

Instructions:
Combine sugar, shortening & salt in a large mixing bowl. Scald milk & pour over sugar mixture. Cool slightly. Meanwhile, soften yeast in a small bowl with warm water (105F to 115F). Add egg, mix slightly. Pour yeast mixture into milk mixture & stir together. Stir in flour till well mixed. Cover dough with a towel. Set aside to rise till doubled in

bulk, about 2 hr. Lightly grease two loaf pans. Punch dough down & knead briefly on a floured surface adding more flour as needed to prevent sticking. Divide in half & shape into loaf pans. Let rise till doubled in bulk again, about 2 hr. Preheat oven to 375F. Bake loaves till lightly browned on top, 20--30 min.

Cooking Tips:

To make it easier to spread sandwich fillings on fresh bread, freeze the dough before assembling the sandwiches. This is a great trick when making sandwiches before work/school because the bread will be thawed entirely well before lunchtime!

Prep time: 45 min **Cook time:** 90 min

Nutritional info: Calories 69 | Total Fat 0.9g | Cholesterol 0mg | Sodium 132mg | Potassium 69.44mg | Carbohydrates 11.6g | Dietary Fiber 1.9g | Sugars 1.6g | Protein 3.6g

BASIC SWEET BREAD
CATEGORIES: BREAD, SWEET

Ingredients:
1/4 cup sugar
1 pkg. active dry yeast
1/2 tsp salt
1/2 cup lukewarm water
1 tsp sugar
3 Cup five roses AF flour
1/2 cup milk
1 egg beaten
2 tbsp. butter
1/2 tsp grated lemon rind

Instructions:
Put milk in saucepan scald add sugar butter & salt (cold to lukewarm). Follow your normal bread, making orders. Your wet ingredients then your dry ones & last put in the yeast. Try this one it works on my bread maker. It is a west bend.

Prep Time: 8 min   **Cook Time:** 25 min
Nutritional Info: Calories 137.5 | Total Fat 1.8 g | Cholesterol 0.8 mg | Sodium 80.7 mg | Potassium 63.9 mg

| Total Carbohydrate 27.2 g | Dietary Fiber 0.8 g | Sugars 7.9 g | Protein 3.3 g

ALMOND BUTTER COOKIES
CATEGORIES: COOKIE, ALMOND

Ingredients:
1/4 cup Canola Oil
1/4 Cup Almond butter
1/4 cup Maple syrup
1/2 tsp vanilla extract
1/4 tsp Salt
1 Cup Whole wheat pastry flour Sifted before measuring

Instructions:
Lightly grease a baking sheet/use a nonstick one. Mix almond butter & oil. Beat till smooth. Mix in maple syrup & vanilla extract. Stir together flour & salt. Add to almond butter mixture & mix till just combined. Cover & refrigerate for 10 Min. Roll dough into 3/4" balls. Place on a baking sheet & flatten with a fork. Bake in 300F oven for 25 min till bottoms are lightly browned. Cool for a couple of Minutes on the baking sheet transfer to a cooling rack.

Prep Time: 10 min   **Cook Time:** 35 min
Nutritional Info: Calories 76.8 | Total Fat 6.4 g | Cholesterol 0.0 mg | Sodium 11.0 mg | Potassium 10.8 mg | Total Carbohydrate 2.4 g | Dietary Fiber 1.6 g | Sugars

0.8 g | Protein 3.4 g

BETTY CROCKER BROWNIES
CATEGORIES: COOKIE, BROWNIE

Ingredients:
1 tsp salt
4 Oz Unsweetened chocolate
2 Cups sugar
2/3 Cup shortening
1 Cup chopped nuts
4 eggs
1 tsp Vanilla
1 ¼ Cups flour
1 tsp baking powder

Instructions:
Preheat oven to 350F. Grease 13 X 9 X 2" pan. Melt chocolate & shortening in a large saucepan over low heat. Remove from heat & stir in sugar, eggs & vanilla. Stir in remaining ingredients. Spread in pan. Bake 30 min/till it starts to pull away from sides of the pan. Cool slightly & cut into bars 2 X 1 1/2". Spread with glossy frosting.

Prep Time: 15 min **Cook Time:** 35 min
Nutritional Info: Calories 190.0 | Total Fat 8.0 g | Cholesterol 25.0 mg | Sodium 125.0 mg | Potassium 100.0 mg | Total Carbohydrate 27.0 g | Dietary Fiber 1.0 g | Sugars 19.0 g | Protein 2.0 g

BUTTERMILK BISCUITS
CATEGORIES: COOKIE, BUTTERMILK

Ingredients:
2 Cup flour
3 1/2 tsp cream of tartar
1/2 tbsp. Salt
1/2 cup (1/4 lb.) Cultured Butter
2 tsp baking soda
2/3 Cup Buttermilk

Instructions:
Preheat oven to 425F. Grease a cookie sheet, flour a work surface. Run the tartar & soda through a strainer to grind out the lumps. Sift dry ingredients together. Cut the butter into the flour. Mix wet & dry together, stirring only till mixed. Knead with a light touch 14 times. Roll or pat dough flat on a floured surface, till 3/4" thick. Cut with a juice glass into 2" rounds. Place on a greased pan, paint tops with some melted butter or milk. Bake for 12--15 min till golden. Serve with Butter, Clabber, Chocolate butter & jam.

Prep Time: 12 min   **Cook Time:** 30 min

Nutritional Info: Calories 178.3 | Total Fat 4.7 g | Cholesterol 1.4 mg | Sodium 37.5 mg | Potassium 91.1 mg | Total Carbohydrate 28.9 g | Dietary Fiber 1.0 g | Sugars 1.8 g | Protein 4.8 g

CARROT DROP COOKIES
CATEGORIES: COOKIE, CARROT

Ingredients:
1 tsp baking powder
2 stiffly beaten egg whites
1/2 tsp ginger
1/2 tsp pumpkin pie spice
1 Cup flour
1/2 carrots cooked & mashed
1/3 cup raisins
2 tsp grated orange rind
1/3 cup chopped dates

Instructions:
Fold carrots & orange rind through stiffly beaten egg whites. In a separate bowl, add baking powder, ginger & pumpkin pie spice to flour; mix well. Fold flour mixture through egg white mixture. Fold in raisins & dates. Drop from a rounded tsp onto a non-stick cookie sheet. Bake at 350F for 15 min/till lightly browned around the edges.

Prep Time: 15 min   Cook Time: 20 min
Nutritional Info: Calories 110.9 | Total Fat 5.6 g |
Cholesterol 0.0 mg | Sodium 164.7 mg | Potassium 41.8
mg | Total Carbohydrate 14.1 g | Dietary Fiber 0.5 g |
Sugars 0.4 g | Protein 1.4 g

CHOCOLATE CHEW
CATEGORIES: COOKIE, CHOCOLATE

Ingredients:
6 Oz butter
1 tbsp. Golden syrup.
1 Cup flour
1 Cup rice bubbles
1 Cup coconut
3/4 Cup sugar
1 tbsp. Cocoa
1/2 tsp vanilla.

Instructions:
Melt together 6 Oz butter & 1 tbsp. Golden syrup. Add 1 cup flour, 1 Cup rice bubbles, 1 Cup coconut, 3/4 cup sugar, 1 tbsp. cocoa & 1/2 tsp vanilla. Mix well together. Bake in medium oven 350F 20 min. Ice with chocolate icing while warm & cut into fingers.

Prep Time: 16 min   **Cook Time:** 25 min
Nutritional Info: Calories 20.0 | Total Fat 0.5 g | Cholesterol 0.0 mg | Sodium 10.0 mg | Potassium 0.0 mg | Total Carbohydrate 3.0 g | Dietary Fiber 0.0 g | Sugars 3.0 g | Protein 0.0 g

DATE-NUT SCONES COOKIE
CATEGORIES: COOKIE, DATE

Ingredients:
1/4 cup maple sugar
1 1/3 cup unbleached white flour
1 tbsp. Lima Yannoh
1 Cup whole wheat pastry flour
2 tsp baking powder
1/2 cup pitted, snipped dates
1 tsp baking soda
1/4 cup coarsely chopped pecans
1/2 tsp Salt
1/2 tsp ground cardamom
2 tbsp. Safflower Oil
3/4 Cup Edensoy mixed with 1 tbsp. Vinegar
2 tbsp. Applesauce

Instructions:
Preheat the oven to 425F. Line a baking sheet with parchment. In a large bowl, mix the first 10 ingredients. In a liquid measuring C, mix the Edensoy-vinegar mixture, oil, & applesauce. Stir the wet ingredients into the dry, just till

moistened. Turn dough out onto a floured board. Dust hands with flour & pat dough into a disk about 1" thick. Cut into 8 wedges & transfer to the baking sheet. Bake till a cake tester comes out dry, about 15 min. Serve warm.

Prep Time: 20 min   **Cook Time:** 20 min
Nutritional Info: Calories 255.4 | Total Fat 11.0 g | Cholesterol 32.5 mg | Sodium 345.5 mg | Potassium 161.3 mg | Total Carbohydrate 38.5 g | Dietary Fiber 5.8 g | Sugars 11.7 g | Protein 7.0 g

FARINA COOKIES
CATEGORIES: COOKIE, GREEK

Ingredients:
COOKIES:
1 Cup Oil
1 Cup Flour
1 Cup Sugar
2 Cup Farina Cream of Wheat
1 Cup Cognace
1 Cup Chopped walnuts
1 Cup Orange juice
1 tsp Cinnamon
1 Cup Sugar
1 tsp Baking powder
2 tbsp. grated orange rind
THE SYRUP:
1 Cup Water
1 Cup Honey
1 Cup Sugar

Instructions:

Beat oil with sugar for 1/2 hr. Add cognac & baking soda dissolved in orange juice & orange rind mix well. Add flour & farina & knead very well to blend all ingredients into a med soft dough. Shape the melomakarona into mounded ovals flat on the bottom. Scrape the top lightly with a fork to make shallow grooves. Place on buttered cookie sheet & bake in 250F oven for 20--30 min. Remove from the oven cold. Boil water sugar & honey together in a saucepan. Remove the froth as it rises. Boil for about 3 min. Dip cold cookies into the warm syrup using a slotted spoon. Remove carefully & drain. Place on a clean platter & sprinkle with the walnuts. Mix the cinnamon & sugar & sprinkle on top.

Prep Time: 10 min   **Cook Time:** 40 min

Nutritional Info: Calories 40 | Total Fat 0.1g | Cholesterol 0mg | Sodium 0mg | Total Carbohydrate 8.5g | Dietary Fiber 0.2g | Sugars 0g | Protein 1.2g

GRAHAM CRACKERS
CATEGORIES: COOKIE, GRAHAM

Ingredients:
2 Cup whole wheat flour
1 cup regular flour
1 tsp baking powder
1/2 tsp baking soda
1/4 tsp salt
1/2 cup shortening
1/2 cup white sugar
1 cup light brown sugar packed
1 tsp vanilla
1/2 cup milk

Instructions:
Stir together flours, baking powder, baking soda, & salt. Cream shortening & sugars till fluffy. Add vanilla. Add flour mixture, alternately with milk, mixing well after each addition. Chill dough till firm. Several hr./overnight. Divide dough into quarters. Roll out each portion on a floured surface to rectangle one-eighth" thick. Trim to 5x15" rectangle. Cut into six 2 1/2" x 5" rectangles. Make a line

down the center of each strip with the back edge of a knife. Mark each 2 1/2" piece with prongs of a fork. Place on greased baking sheets. Bake in a preheated oven at 350F for 10 to 12 mins, or till crisp & edges are browned. Remove immediately from baking sheets & cool on wire racks.

Prep Time: 15 min   **Cook Time:** 20 min
Nutritional Info: Calories 423 | Total Fat 10g | Cholesterol 0mg | Sodium 477mg | Potassium 135mg | Total Carbohydrate 77g | Dietary fiber 2.8g | Sugar 31g | Protein 7g

CHEESE HAM CASSEROLE
CATEGORIES: CHEESE, HAM

Ingredients:
1 pkg. Green beans, French cut (10oz)
4 tbsp. Butter
1/4 cup Onion, minced
4 tbsp. Flour, all-purpose
1/2 tsp Salt
1 ½ Cup Milk
2 Cup Ham, cooked, chopped
2 Eggs, hard-cooked, chopped
1 Cup Cheddar cheese, shredded (4oz)
2 tbsp. Pimiento, chopped
1 tbsp. Parsley, chopped
1/2 Cup Croutons, herb-flavored, crush

Instructions:
Cook beans according to pkg direction. Drain & reserve 1/2 C liquid. Melt butter in a 2-qt saucepan sautés onion. Stir in flour & salt till well blended. Remove from heat stir in milk & reserved 1/2 C liquid. Heat to a boil, stirring steadily boil

& stir 1 min. Remove from heat stir in ham, eggs, cheese, pimiento, and parsley. Place beans in baking dish cover with ham sauce & sprinkle croutons over the top. Bake in preheated 350F oven 20--25 min.

Prep Time: 20 min   **Cook Time:** 45 min
Nutritional Info: Calories 425.4 | Total Fat 12.1g | Cholesterol 74.9mg | Sodium 2,085.6mg | Potassium 683.7 mg | Total Carbohydrate 43.8g | Dietary Fiber 5.0g | Sugars 1.1g | Protein 37.2g

CHEESY RICE RAMEKINS
CATEGORIES: RICE, CHEESE, EGG

Ingredients:
4 tbsp. Butter
4 tbsp. Parmesan cheese grated
2 small Mozzarella cheeses chopped
3 eggs beaten
2 tbsp. fresh breadcrumbs
1 Cup Rice
2 Cup Water

Instructions:
Cook rice in boiling water for 15 min/till tender. Drain. Add half butter & half parmesan cheese together with all the Mozzarella & eggs. Mix well. Grease the ramekin dishes with half the remaining butter. Then coat evenly with the breadcrumbs. Pack the prepared ramekins with the rice mixture, top with dots of the remaining butter & Parmesan cheese & bake in a preheated oven at 450F for 15 min. Serve with ratatouille for a vegetarian meal.

Prep Time: 15 min   **Cook Time:** 26 min
Nutritional Info: Calories 180 | Total Carbs 37g | Dietary Fiber 1g | Sugar 3g | Total Fat 12g | Protein 6g | Sodium 810mg | Potassium 0mg | Cholesterol 5mg

CHUNKY CHEESE BREAD
CATEGORIES: CHEESE, BREAD

Ingredients:
1 tbsp. green onion (sliced)
1/4 cup sun-dried tomatoes (chopped)
8 Oz Jalapeño-Jack cheese (cubed)
1 lb. hot roll mix + ingredients to make a mix

Instructions:
Make hot roll mix to pkg. Directions, adding sun-dried tomatoes & green onion. Knead cheese into the dough. Divide dough in half; shape into 2 round/oval loaves on a greased cookie sheet. Let rise (covered), in a warm place till doubled in size, 30--40 min. Bake at 375F till golden, about 20 min.

Prep Time: 20 min   **Cook Time:** 60 min
Nutritional Info: Calories 71 | Total Fat 1.24g | Cholesterol 1mg | Sodium 176mg | Total Carbohydrate

12.52g | Dietary Fiber 0.6g | Sugars 1.07g | Protein 2.21g

AVOCADO ANGEL EGGS
CATEGORIES: EGG, AVOCADO

Ingredients:
12 eggs
2 ripe California avocados, medium
1 tsp capers
2 tbsp. shallots minced
1 tbsp. lemon juice
1/2 tsp paprika
6 black Nicoise olives, diced

Instructions:
Boil the eggs for 3 min. Peel & slice each egg in half lengthwise. Remove egg yolks & place the egg white halves on a serving platter. Puree avocados & fold in minced shallots, mashed capers & lemon. Pipe mixture from a pastry pipette bag/spoon mixture into the egg whites. Garnish with a sprinkle of paprika & diced olives.

Prep Time: 5 min   **Cook Time:** 15 min
Nutritional Info: Calories 254.4 | Total Fa 17.8 g | Cholesterol 213.0 mg | Sodium 551.8 mg | Potassium 600.5 mg | Total Carbohydrate 8.4 g | Dietary Fiber 5.9 g |

Sugars 0.9 g | Protein 15.3 g

BREAKFAST CASSEROLE A BAKED EGG, SAUSAGE, & BREAD CASSEROLE
CATEGORIES: EGG, SAUSAGE

Ingredients:
8 large eggs
2 ½ Cup milk
3 Cup bread cubes
1 tsp dry mustard
2 lb. Bulk sausage
1 lb. grated cheddar (or more to taste)
1/2 lb. fresh mushrooms

Instructions:
Brown the sausage in a frying pan; drain off excess fat. Set aside. In a large bowl, beat the eggs. Add milk, mustard, & bread cubes. If you like salty dishes, add a tsp of salt. Wait a few mins for the bread cubes to absorb the milk & eggs. Stir in 80% of the grated cheese. Add the cooked & drained sausage. Mix well. Pour into a casserole dish of the size that

you would use to make lasagna (about 9x13"). Slice the mushrooms, & arrange the slices on top of the casserole. Sprinkle the remaining 20% of the cheese over the top of the mushrooms. Bake for 45 min at 350F. Let cool 10 min before serving.

Prep Time: 20 min   **Cook Time:** 50 min
Nutritional Info: Calories 223.6 | Total Fat 15.4 g | Cholesterol 143.0 mg | Sodium 460.9 mg | Potassium 169.5 mg | Total Carbohydrate 7.6 g | Dietary Fiber 0.6 g | Sugars 0.7 g | Protein 13.2 g

BREAKFAST CASSEROLE
CATEGORIES: EGG, SAUSAGE, POTATO

Ingredients:
1 pkg. Gimme Lean Sausage
1 pkg. Simply Shreds/other FF hash browns
4-6 Egg Beaters
8 oz pkg. of shredded FF cheddar cheese

Instructions:
Brown hash browns & Gimme Lean in a nonstick skillet (may cook together, separately if you want distinct layers). Season potatoes with S/P. Put hash browns & Gimme Lean in 8x13" nonstick cake pan. Pour eggs over the layers/mixture. Spread cheese shreds over the top. Bake in 350/375F preheated oven for 45 min/till egg is cooked & cheese browned.

Prep Time: 10 min   **Cook Time:** 20 min
Nutritional Info: Calories 140.0 | Total Fat 5.9 g |
Cholesterol 17.7 mg | Sodium 340.6 mg | Potassium 48.0
mg | Total Carbohydrate 11.5 g | Dietary Fiber 0.8 g |
Sugars 2.8 g | Protein 10.7 g

HAM CASSEROLE
CATEGORIES: EGG

Ingredients:
12 slices white bread buttered
3 Cup Ham diced
1/2 lb. Processed pasteurized cheese such as Velveeta diced pkg.
14 Oz Baby Broccoli Florets
6 eggs well beaten
¼ cup milk
1 tsp salt
1/2 tsp pepper
1 tsp dry mustard

Instructions:
Cut bread into cubes & place into well-oiled 9x13" casserole dish. Add ham, cheese, & broccoli. In a medium mixing bowl, beat eggs & milk. Add mustard, S/P & mix well. Pour over bread. Refrigerate overnight/allow the bread to soak into the egg mixture. Bake, uncovered for 1 hr. in 350F oven.

Prep Time: 20 min   **Cook Time:** 70 min

Nutritional Info: Calories 292.5 | Total Fat 15.9 g | Cholesterol 61.2 mg | Sodium 1,036.0 mg | Potassium 304.4 mg | Total Carbohydrate 21.7 g | Dietary Fiber 0.7 g | Sugars 0.2 g | Protein 15.5 g

BREAKFAST SAUSAGE CASSEROLE
CATEGORIES: EGG, QUICHE

Ingredients:
16 Oz pkg. Jimmy Dean Sausage cooked/crumbled
4 Oz cheddar cheese shredded
10 eggs slightly beaten
4 Oz Swiss cheese shredded
3 Cup light cream
1 bn. green onions chopped
1 tsp salt
16 Oz day-old bread cubed
1 tsp dry mustard

Instructions:
Grease 9"x 13" pan well. Place bread in a pan. Sprinkle with cheeses & sausage. Combine rest of ingredients together & mix well. Pour over bread refrigerate overnight. Bake for 1 hr. at 350F/till golden brown.

Prep Time: 20 min   **Cook Time:** 75 min

Nutritional Info: Calories 334 | Total Carbs 13 g | Dietary Fiber 0 g | Sugar 0g | Total Fat 23 g | Protein 17 g | Sodium 631 mg | Potassium 0 mg | Cholesterol 222 mg

BREAKFAST TORTILLA STRATA
CATEGORIES: EGG

Ingredients:
1 Cup salsa
1 Cup can black beans, rinsed & drained
Cooking spray
10 (6") corn tortillas in 1" strips
4 Oz shredded Monterey Jack cheese
1 Cup FF milk
1/2 tsp salt
2 large eggs
1 Cup LF sour cream
2 large egg whites
1/4 cup thinly sliced green onions

Instructions:
Mix salsa & beans in a bowl. Put 1/3 tortilla strips in an 11x7" baking dish coated with cooking spray. Top with 1/3 Cup cheese & about 1 cup salsa mixture. Repeat procedure with 1/3 tortilla strips, 1/3 Cup cheese, & remaining salsa mixture. Top with remaining tortilla strips. Combine sour cream & next 4 ingredients (sour cream through egg whites).

Stir with a whisk. Stir in onions. Pour over tortilla strip
sprinkle with 1/3 Cup cheese. Cover & chill 8
hr./overnight. Preheat oven to 350F. Remove dish from
refrigerator. Let stand at room temp 10 min. Cover & bake
at 350F for 20 min. Uncover & bake an additional 15
min/till lightly browned.

Prep Time: 20 min   **Cook Time:** 26 min
Nutritional Info: Calories 292 | Total Fat 9.2g | Protein
17.7g | Total Carbohydrate 36.5g | Fiber 4.7g | Cholesterol
93mg | Sodium 755mg | Calcium 335mg

LUNCH MEALS

APPLE BEEF CHILI
CATEGORIES: BEAN, CHILI, BEEF

Ingredients:
1-1/2 lb. lean ground beef
4 medium onions, chopped (2 Cups)

3 cl Garlic, minced
29 Oz can tomatoes, cut up
15 Oz can tomato sauce
14-1/2 Oz can chicken broth
3 tbsp. Chili powder
2 tbsp. unsweetened cocoa powder
1 tbsp. curry powder
8 Oz can diced green chili peppers, drained
1 tsp ground cinnamon
15 Oz can red kidney beans, drained
2/3 cup slivered almonds
3 green, red, &/yellow sweet peppers chop
2-1/4 Cup Raisins, cheddar cheese, & plain yogurt/dairy sour cream (optional)
2 cooking apples (such as Granny Smith/Jonathan), cored & chopped (about 2 Cups)

Instructions:

In a large Dutch oven cook beef, onions, & garlic till meat is brown. Drain off fat. Stir in undrained tomatoes, tomato sauce, broth, peppers, green chili peppers, apples, chili powder, cocoa, curry, & cinnamon. Bring to boiling reduce heat. Cover simmer for 1 hr. Add kidney beans & almonds. Heat through. Serve with raisins, cheddar cheese, & yogurt/sour cream, if desired.

Prep Time: 20 min   **Cook Time:** 75 min
Nutritional Info: Calories 287.2 | Total Fat 12.6 g | Cholesterol 42.4 mg | Sodium 768.0 mg | Potassium 490.7 mg | Total Carbohydrate 27.7 g | Dietary Fiber 10.5 g | Sugars 6.3 g | Protein 17.2 g

BASIC BEAN BURGERS
CATEGORIES: BEAN, BURGER

Ingredients:
Scant cup boiling water
1 tbsp. tomato paste or ketchup
2 cl garlic minced
16 Oz can pinto or other beans, drained
1/2 tsp oregano
1 tbsp. Tamari/soy sauce
1 tsp sweetener
1/4 Cup whole wheat bread crumbs
S/P to taste
Whole-wheat flour for dusting
1 Cup TVP granules (this is a textured vegetable protein.

Instructions:
Pour boiling water over TVP & tomato paste in a bowl. Stir & let rest for 10 min. In a food processor, combine TVP mixture & remaining ingredients except for the flour. Pulse till mixture is almost a puree. Dust hands with flour & shape mixture into 6 burgers. Dust them lightly in flour. Layer the burgers with sheets of waxed paper & refrigerate for at least 1 hr. Cook on a grill covered with foil for about 10 min on

each side.

Prep Time: 15 min   **Cook Time:** 75 min
Nutritional Info: Calories 110.0 | Total Fat 4.0 g | Cholesterol 0.0 mg | Sodium 330.0 mg | Potassium 260.0 mg | Total Carbohydrate 13.0 g | Dietary Fiber 4.0 g | Sugars 1.8 g | Protein 10.0 g

BEAN & RICE BURGERS
CATEGORIES: BEAN, BURGER, RICE, FLOUR

Ingredients:
1 Cup Cooked brown rice
1 1/2 Cup Cooked beans pink, kidney, navy, etc.
1/2 cup Wheat flour/white
1 tbsp. Margarine/butter
1 medium Onion, diced
1 Cl Garlic, mashed
1 tbsp. Spike/seasoning salt

OPTIONAL:
1 Cup Cooked mashed potatoes
1/2 Cup Cornmeal
1/2 Cup Bran
1/2 Cup Cracked wheat
1 small Pepper, diced
1 Grated carrot

Instructions:
Heat greased grill/electric frypan on medium heat. Or, you can grease a 13"x9" glass baking pan & bake at 350F 30 Min.

Just spread the mix in a pan & cook uncovered. Use a pancake turner to cut & remove cooked 'burger.' Mash beans. Add all ingredients & mix well. (If you use all of the ingredients listed your mix may be a bit dry. You might want to add a 1/4 to 1/2 Cup of soy, nut/rice milk. Of course, you also could use whole milk. Be sure you don't think it too much/it will be mushy. Look for a 'hamburger' consistency.) Spoon about 2 heaping tbsp. of mix onto grill/fry pan for each burger. Flatten with greased pancake turner. Turn several times rather than just once on each side like conventional burgers; they have a better texture that way.

Prep Time: 15 min   **Cook Time:** 50 min
Nutritional Info: Calories 154.8 | Total Fat 2.0 g | Cholesterol 0.0 mg | Sodium 139.7 mg | Potassium 68.7 mg | Total Carbohydrate 27.8 g | Dietary Fiber 6.1 g | Sugars 1.0 g | Protein 6.3 g

BEAN CASSEROLE
CATEGORIES: BEAN, BAKED, LENTIL

Ingredients:
1 can lentils
1 tsp each garlic powder, oregano, basil
1 can kidney beans
1 small can tomatoes (diced)
S/P to taste
1/2 cup grated soy cheese

Instructions:
Drain liquid off the lentils, & mix with kidney beans (not drained) in a casserole dish. Drain about 2/3 the juice from the tomatoes, & add to the beans. It is essential to do this because it gets too "soupy" if there is too much liquid. Add soy cheese & seasoning. Bake in 350F oven for 30--45 min (till heated through).

Prep Time: 12 min   **Cook Time:** 50 min
Nutritional Info: Calories 223.9 | Total Fat 8.2 g | Cholesterol 28.4 mg | Sodium 471.7 mg | Potassium 466.0 mg | Total Carbohydrate 26.7 g | Dietary Fiber 6.1 g | Sugars 5.3 g | Protein 11.7 g

All Day Recipe: Think A Complete Meal

BEAN CURD ROLLS

CATEGORIES: BEAN, CURD, ONION, ASPARAGUS, RICE, MUSHROOM, NUT

Ingredients:
1 tbsp. Vegetable oil
1 Cup Uncooked short grain rice
1 Garlic clove, minced
1/2 small Carrot, cut into 1" slivers
2 Green onions, sliced
6 Dried shiitake mushrooms
1 tbsp. Hoisin sauce
1/4 Cup Slivered bamboo shoots
2 tbsp. Soy sauce
1/4 Cup Ginkgo nuts, optional
2 tsp Rice wine/dry sherry
2 Pitted dates, chopped
2 tsp Sesame oil
6 Dried bean curd sheets, soaked for a few mins
6 tbsp. Vegetable oil

1 tbsp. Flour mixed with 1 tbsp. water
3 Asparagus tips, cut into 1/2" pieces, diagonally

Instructions:
Cover rice with warm water & soak for 30 min. Drain. Line
the inside of a steamer with a damp cheesecloth. Place rice
on the cheesecloth. Then cover & steam the rice over
boiling water for 30 min. Set aside. Meanwhile, cover
mushrooms with warm water & soak for 30 min. Drain well.
Cut off & discard stems. Thinly slice caps. Set aside. Place a
wok over high heat till hot. Add oil, swirling to coat sides.
Add garlic & cook, stirring for 10 sec. Add carrot &
asparagus & stir fry for 2 min. Add reserved mushrooms,
bamboo shoots, nuts, dates, onions, hoisin sauce, soy sauce,
rice wine/sherry & sesame oil. Stir fry for 2 min. Add rice
& mix well. Transfer to a bowl & set aside.
To Make Rolls:
Spread about 2 heaping tbsp. of filling diagonally across a
bean curd sheet. Keep remaining sheets covered to prevent
drying. Fold bottom corner over filling to cover, then fold
over right & left corners. Rollover once to enclose filling.
Brush sides & top of the triangle with flour & water mixture.
Fold over to seal. Cover filled rolls with a damp cloth while
preparing the rest of the rolls. Place a non-stick frying pan
over medium heat. Add 1 to 2 tbsp. oil. Add rolls two at a
time & cook for 2 min on each side/till golden brown.
Transfer to a heatproof dish & keep warm in a 200F oven
while cooking remaining rolls. To serve, cut each roll into
thirds.

Prep Time: 45 min   **Cook Time:** 85 min
Nutritional Info: Calories 87 | Total Carbs 3 g | Dietary
Fiber 1 g | Sugar 2 g | Total Fat 5 g | Protein 6 g | Sodium
186 mg | Potassium 0 mg | Cholesterol 0 mg

BEAN CURRY
CATEGORIES: BEAN, CURRY

Ingredients:
1 medium onion, sliced
1--2 hot green Chilies, sliced
1 cl Garlic crushed
5--6 Curry leaves & Rampe pieces (optional)
1 tbsp. Raw curry powder
1/2 tsp Fenugreek seeds
1/4 tsp Turmeric
1/2 Cup thick Coconut milk (or fresh milk)
1 tbsp. Vegetable oil
Salt & Lime juice to taste
1 lb. Beans cut into pieces.

Instructions:
Heat oil in a saucepan. Add onions, green chilies, garlic & curry leaves. Fry until the onions are golden brown. Add the curry powder, salt, turmeric & fenugreek seeds. Stir and fry for 2--3 min. Add cut beans & mix well till beans are well

coated with the curry powder mix. Reduce heat & allow the beans to cook. Add coconut milk (or fresh milk) & allow to simmer for a few more mins. Add a dash of lime juice. Taste & adjust salt

Prep Time: 0 min   **Cook Time:** 15 min
Nutritional Info: Calories 127.9 | Total Fat 4.3 g | Cholesterol 0.0 mg | Sodium 457.4 mg | Potassium 431.3 mg | Total Carbohydrate 19.4 g | Dietary Fiber 5.2 g | Sugars 3.2 g | Protein 4.8 g

BEAN PATTIES
CATEGORIES: BEAN, BURGER, PATTIES

Ingredients:
1 small Onion chop
1/4 Cup Parsley chopped
2 Egg yolks
2 tbsp. cream or evaporated milk
1/4 tsp pepper
1 tsp salt
Flour
Margarine
2 Cup Beans cooked

Instructions:
Beat together the first 4 ingredients Shape into balls Flatten them. Dip them in flour. Chill the patties for one or more hr. Sauté slowly in margarine till brown. Serve with barbecue or other sauce.

Prep Time: 0 min   **Cook Time:** 15 min
Nutritional Info: Calories115 481 | Total Fat 3.8g | Cholesterol 0.7mg mg | Sodium 348mg | Potassium 255mg

| Total Carbohydrate 13.2g | Dietary Fiber 4.6g | Sugars 1.9g | Protein 10.8g

CHILE BEANS
CATEGORIES: BEAN, CHILI

Ingredients:
1 lb. ground beef
1/2 onion, diced
1 tbsp. Shortening
2 tbsp. flour
3 tsp powder red chili
1/2 Cup of the bean juice
2--3 cl garlic

Instructions:
Brown 1 lb. ground beef with 1/2 onion, diced. In a skillet add about 1 tbsp. shortening with about 2 tbsp. Flour. Brown, then add about 3 tsp powder red chili. Have about 1/2 C of the bean juice to stir lightly to chili as you transfer immediately to beans, to avoid burning the chili. Stir beans really good to avoid the beans becoming lumpy. Add cooked ground beef, 2--3 cl garlic, minced. Let simmer for a while, about 15 min.

Prep Time: 5 min   **Cook Time:** 20 min
Nutritional Info: Calories 280.0 | Total Fat 9.0 g |
Cholesterol 66.0 mg | Sodium 1,183.0 mg | Potassium
546.0 mg | Total Carbohydrate 22.0 g | Dietary Fiber 7.0 g
| Sugars 6.0 g | Protein 30.0 g

CHILI NACHOS
CATEGORIES: BEAN, BEEF, ONION, PASTA SAUCE, CHEESE

Ingredients:
1 medium onion, chopped
1 ½ lb. lean ground beef
2 tbsp. chili powder
jar (26 Oz) Ragu(r) Pasta Sauce Traditional
Tortilla chips
1 Cup shredded cheddar cheese (4 Oz)
A can 19 Oz red kidney beans
2 ¼ Cup rinsed & drained

Instructions:
In 12" skillet, brown ground beef with onion & chili powder over medium-high heat, stirring occasionally. Stir in beans & Pasta Sauce. Bring to boil over high heat. Reduce heat to low & simmer covered, stirring occasionally, 20 min. Spoon over tortilla chips, then top with cheese.

Prep Time: 8 min   **Cook Time:** 30 min
Nutritional Info: Calories 219 | Total Fat 10.65g | Cholesterol 20mg | Sodium 669mg | Total Carbohydrate 25.9g | Dietary Fiber 5.9g | Sugars 1.68g Protein 7.93g

CREOLE BEAN PATTIES
CATEGORIES: SANDWICH, BURGER, BEAN

Ingredients:
4 Cup cooked red/pink beans, drained
1/4 tsp cayenne
4 green onions, sliced thin
Tabasco to taste
1/2 red bell pepper, chopped
1/2 tsp thyme
1/2 cup chopped fresh parsley
1/4 tsp garlic powder
about 1/2 cup apple fiber

Instructions:
In a food processor/blender, combine beans, onions, red pepper, parsley, cayenne, Tabasco, thyme, garlic powder, & 1/4 Cup of the apple fiber. Process till smooth. Place remaining apple fiber in a shallow bowl. Dipping your hands in the apple fiber, shape the bean puree into patties about 2 1/2" diameter & 3/4" thick. Spray a skillet with

Pam/Baker's Joy & heat. Cook patties for 5 min on each side.

Prep Time: 0 min   **Cook Time:** 20 min
Nutritional Info: Calories 305.3 | Total Fat 9.9 g | Cholesterol 0.0 mg | Sodium 1,147.6 mg | Potassium 237.6 mg | Total Carbohydrate 43.0 g | Dietary Fiber 11.5 g | Sugars 3.8 g | Protein 12.8 g

3 SOUP CROCKPOT ROASTS
CATEGORIES: SOUP, MUSHROOM, CHEESE

Ingredients:
1 chuck roast
2 can golden mushroom soup
soup carrots
1 can French onion
2 can Cheddar cheese soup

Instructions:
Add all soup to crockpot & mix well, DO NOT ADD WATER! Brown roast, add to soup mixture. Cook on high 5 hr. Add carrots, cook another 2 hr. till very tender. Serve with Mashed potatoes.

Prep Time: 15 min   **Cook Time:** 5 hr
Nutritional Info: Calories 292.7 | Total Fat 17.8 g | Cholesterol 54.0 mg | Sodium 630.5 mg | Potassium 444.1 mg | Total Carbohydrate 5.9 g | Dietary Fiber 0.6 g | Sugars 0.8 g | Protein 25.4 g

All Day Recipe: Think A Complete Meal

⌐ DIFFERENT CHICKEN NOODLE SOUP
CATEGORIES: SOUP, NOODLE

Ingredients:
3 carrots peeled
1 small sweet potato peeled
4 ribs celery sliced
1 small parsnip peeled & sliced
Sprigs fresh dill
4 lb. boneless skinless chicken breast
Pepper to taste
8 Oz thin egg noodles cooked & drained

Instructions:
Place chicken, vegetables & dill in a large kettle. Add water to cover, about 2 1/2 gt. Cover & bring to a boil over high heat. Skim foam from top as needed. Add pepper; cover & simmer for 2 hr. Remove the chicken & vegetables; set aside to cool. Pour the broth through a strainer; skim fat. Slice carrots & diced chicken; return to broth. Add cooked noodles to soup & heat through.

Prep Time: 20 min   **Cook Time:** 2 hrs
Nutritional info: Calories 351.3 | Total Fat 4.5 g |

Cholesterol 92.7 mg | Sodium 1,168.8 mg | Potassium 1,263.2 mg | Total Carbohydrate 37.3 g | Dietary Fiber 6.1 g | Sugars 5.1 g | Protein 39.7 g

ACORN SQUASH SOUP
CATEGORIES: SOUP, SQUASH

Ingredients:
1 onion, diced
1--1 1/2 tsp mace/to taste
2 tbsp. Butter
Cinnamon for garnish
1/2 cup dry sherry
6 cup chicken stock/can chicken broth
S/P
2 cup heavy cream
2 Acorn Squash, peeled, seeded in large dice

Instructions:
In a large saucepan set over medium heat, cook the onion in the butter, occasionally stirring, for 3 min. Add the sherry & mace & reduce liquid by half. Add the stock, squash, & S/P. Bring liquid to a boil & simmer, occasionally stirring, for 1 hr. Add the heavy cream & return soup to the simmer. Remove from heat. In a blender, puree the soup in batches, then return it to the saucepan. Correct seasoning to taste. Ladle soup into bowls & garnish with a sprinkling of

cinnamon.

Prep Time: 5 min **Cook Time:** 80 min
Nutritional Info: Calories 231.7 | Total Fat 18.6 g |
Cholesterol 54.1 mg | Sodium 753.4 mg | Potassium 609.5
mg | Total Carbohydrate 15.2 g | Dietary Fiber 3.4 g |
Sugars 0.9 g | Protein 3.7 g

ALASKAN CLAM CHOWDER
CATEGORIES: SOUP, CLAM, ONION, MILK, POTATO

Ingredients:
1 large onion diced
Nectar clams/a can of nectar
6 strips bacon
1 tsp onion powder/to taste
1 can milk
5 medium potatoes diced
8 Cup water
4 Cup margarine (optional)
S/P to taste
12 razor clams, coarsely chopped/1 large can clams
1/2 cup long-grain rice

Instructions:
Dice bacon cook till brown & crisp reserve the drippings.
Cook rice in the water about 5 min then add all ingredients

except clams, bacon & milk. Cook an additional 15 min. Turn off heat & add the bacon, clams & 1/4 C bacon drippings margarine may be substituted. Milk may be added to the chowder now/place a container on the table & let each person add their own. Add the milk at the table as it tends to curdle when reheated &, chowder is best the sec day.

Prep Time: 10 min   **Cook Time:** 35 min
Nutritional Info: Calories 191.2 | Total Fat 2.6 g | Cholesterol 19.0 mg | Sodium 374.5 mg | Potassium 852.3 mg | Total Carbohydrate 31.5 g | Dietary Fiber 3.3 g | Sugars 1.1 g | Protein 11.1 g

BARLEY STEW
CATEGORIES: SOUP, BARLEY, STEW

Ingredients:
1 Cup barley, dried
1 large onion, chopped
4 slices of ginger
2 cl Garlic, chopped
2 carrots chopped
4 stalks of celery cut into small pieces
1 small can kidney beans
1 tsp curry powder (optional)
5 Cup water
2--3 potatoes peeled & chopped
2 can whole tomatoes, peeled & cut into chunks

Instructions:
Place barley in a large Pyrex bowl. Add water, cover with plastic wrap. Nuke for 20 min on full power. May need 10 more min till barley is cooked. Sauté onion, garlic, ginger & curry in a nonstick pan. Continue to sauté, adding the

remaining ingredients. Bring to a boil & turn to a simmer. Simmer 30--45 min till potatoes & carrots are cooked. You may have to add more water.

Prep Time: 10 min   **Cook Time:** 28 min
Nutritional Info: Calories 344.3 | Total Fat 8.1 g | Cholesterol 76.8 mg | Sodium 746.6 mg | Potassium 1,057.3 mg | Total Carbohydrate 39.7 g | Dietary Fiber 6.4 g | Sugars 4.8 g | Protein 28.5 g

BEER & CHEESE SOUP

Ingredients:
1 Cup Diced onions
1 Cup Diced celery
1 Cup Diced carrots
1 Cup Diced mushrooms
3/4 Cup Butter
1/2 Cup Flour
1 tsp Dry mustard
5 Cup Chicken/vegetable stock
1 bn. Broccoli
11 fl. Beer (use a can/bottle and save a swallow for the cook!)
6 Oz Cheddar cheese, grated
2 tbsp. Grated Parmesan cheese
S/P

Instructions:
Sauté the diced vegetables in butter. Mix flour and mustard

into fried vegetables. Add the chicken or vegetable stock to mixture & cook for five min. Break broccoli into small flowerets cut stems into bite-sizes pieces. Steam till tender-crisp. Add beer & cheeses to the soup. Simmer 10--15 min. Check seasonings.

To serve: Place some broccoli into a soup bowl & ladle the soup over it.

NOTES: Because of the cheese, this soup doesn't survive a night in the refrigerator very well.

Prep Time: 10 min   **Cook Time**: 36 min
Nutritional Info: Calories 287.4 | Total Fat 22.6 g | Cholesterol 64.8 mg | Sodium 625.2 mg | Potassium 283.9 mg | Total Carbohydrate 7.4 g | Dietary Fiber 0.2 g | Sugars 0.5 g | Protein 11.1 g

CALICO BEAN SOUP
CATEGORIES: SOUP, BEAN

Ingredients:
Pkg. of beans
Packet of spices
2 qt. of water
Hambone, ham hock/1/2 lb. of ham
1 large onion, chopped
28 Oz can of tomatoes
Juice of 1 lemon
Salt to taste

Instructions:
If desired, omit ham & substitute beef, chicken/vegetable stock for the cooking water. Wash beans thoroughly. Put in a kettle, cover with water & soak overnight. Next, drain beans & add 2 qt. of new water & ham/ham hock (or use broth if omitting ham). Simmer slowly for 2 1/2 to 3 hr. Then add spice packet, onion, tomatoes (undrained), lemon juice & salt to taste. Simmer another 30 min/till beans are tender. Take ham from the soup. Remove any bits of ham

from bone & return to soup. If using boneless ham, cut into bite-size pieces & return to soup. Serve.

NOTES: Substitute beans freely use Anasazi beans, pink beans, red beans, etc. There should be approx. 1 lb. of beans in all.

Prep Time: 15 min   **Cook Time:** 52 min
Nutritional Info: Calories 144.5 | Total Fat 4.1 g | Cholesterol 19.4 mg | Sodium 641.0 mg | Potassium 409.3 mg | Total Carbohydrate 16.9 g | Dietary Fiber 5.2 g | Sugars 1.1 g | Protein 10.5 g

CHICKEN TAGINE
CATEGORIES: SOUP, STEW, CHICKEN, OLIVE, TOMATO, PASTA

Ingredients:
1 tsp ground cumin
1/4 cup chopped fresh parsley
1 tsp ground turmeric
1/4 cup chopped fresh cilantro
4 garlic cloves, finely chopped
1/2 cup chicken broth
2 chicken drumsticks (1/2 lb.), skinned
1/4 cup chopped green olives
2 chicken thighs (1/2 lb.), skinned
2 chicken breast halves (3/4 lb.), skinned
1 tbsp. grated lemon rind
1-1/2 tsp fresh lemon juice
1/4 tsp salt
14-1/2 Oz can plum tomatoes, undrained & chopped
4 Cup hot cooked couscous

Cilantro sprigs (optional)

Instructions:
Preheat oven to 400F. Combine first 5 ingredients in a small bowl, & rub over chicken. Put chicken pieces in a 13 x 9" baking dish add broth & the next 5 ingredients. Cover & bake at 400F for 1 hr. till chicken is done. Serve the tagine over couscous, & garnish with cilantro sprigs, if desired.

Prep Time: 15 min   **Cook time:** 65 min
Nutritional Info: Calories 331.1 | Total Fat 16.0 g | Cholesterol 57.1 mg | Sodium 69.6 mg | Potassium 722.8 mg | Total Carbohydrate 33.2 g | Dietary Fiber 5.6 g | Sugars 15.1 g | Protein 17.1 g

EASY CHILI
CATEGORIES: SOUP, CHILI

Ingredients:
3 lb. ground beef
3 cup tomato paste
1 large onion, chopped
1 medium head garlic, peeled & chopped
1 Cup dry black beans
1 cup dry kidney beans
1 Cup dry pinto beans
2 (28 Oz) cans diced tomatoes, drained
8 Oz can tomato sauce
2 tbsp. chili powder, to taste
S/P to taste
1 tsp hot pepper sauce, to taste

Instructions:
In a large pot over medium heat, cook beef, onion & garlic

till meat is brown. Stir in black beans, kid.
beans, tomatoes, tomato paste & tomato sau
chili powder, S/P & pepper sauce. Reduce
simmer 2 to 3 hr., till beans are tender.

Prep Time: 20 min   **Cook Time** ____s
Nutritional Info: Calories 287.2 | Total Fat 12.6 g |
Cholesterol 42.4 mg | Sodium 768.0 mg | Potassium 490.7
mg | Total Carbohydrate 27.7 g | Dietary Fiber 10.5 g |
Sugars 6.3 g | Protein 17.2 g

FISH STEW
CATEGORIES: SOUP, STEW, FISH, CORN, BEAN

Ingredients:
1 lb. red potatoes
10 Oz pkg. frozen green beans with Spaetzle
1 ¼ lb. cod/scrod fillet
14 1/2 Oz can Italian style stewed tomatoes
3/4 tsp salt
10 oz pkg. frozen whole-kernel corn

Instructions:
Cut unpeeled potatoes into 1" chunks. In a 4-qt saucepan over high heat, heat potatoes & 3 cup water to boiling. Reduce heat to low cover & simmer 10 min/till potatoes are almost tender. Meanwhile, cut cod into large chunks. To potatoes & water in a saucepan, add stewed tomatoes, frozen green beans with Spaetzle, & frozen corn. Over high

heat, heat to boiling. Stir in cod & salt heat to boiling. Reduce heat to low. Cover & simmer 5 min/till cod flakes easily when tested with a fork.

Prep Time: 10 min   **Cook Time:** 35 min
Nutritional Info: Calories 173.9 | Total Fat 1.8 g | Cholesterol   76.6 mg | Sodium 292.9 mg | Potassium 698.2 mg | Total Carbohydrate 7.2 g | Dietary Fiber 1.5 g | Sugars 3.5 g | Protein 30.6 g

DINNER MEALS

ALL DAY MACARONI & CHEESE
CATEGORIES: PASTA, CHEESE

Ingredients:
8 Oz elbow macaroni cooked & drained
3 cup sharp Cheddar cheese shredded, (12 Oz)

12 Oz can evaporate milk
1 ½ Cup milk
2 eggs
1 tsp salt
1/2 tsp black pepper
1 cup sharp Cheddar cheese shredded, (4 Oz)

Instructions:
Place the cooked macaroni in a 3 1/2-qt (or large) slow cooker that has been coated with nonstick cooking spray. Add 3 Cup cheese, milk, eggs and seasonings to the macaroni mix well. Sprinkle with the remaining 1 cup cheese, then cover & cook on the low setting for 5--6 hr. till the mixture is firm & golden around the edges. Do not remove the cover/stir till the mixture has finished cooking.

Prep Time: 5 min   **Cook Time:** 6hrs
Nutritional Info: Calories 219.0 | Total Fat 7.0 g | Cholesterol 24.0 mg | Sodium 251.0 mg | Potassium 0.0 mg | Total Carbohydrate 25.0 g | Dietary Fiber 1.0 g | Sugars 4.0 g | Protein 13.0 g

APPLE MINT COUSCOUS (SAUCE FOR LAMB)
CATEGORIES: PASTA, COUSCOUS, MINT, CHEESE, APPLE, SHALLOT

Ingredients:
S/P
1 tbsp. plus 1 tsp butter, in all
1 Cup couscous
1 Cup peeled & finely chopped sweet apples
1 tbsp. Olive oil
1 tbsp. minced shallots
1 Cup chicken stock
2 Oz crumbled feta
Fresh rosemary
1 tsp minced garlic
3 tbsp. chopped fresh mint, plus extra for garnish

Instructions:

In a sauté pan, heat 1 tbsp. of butter. When the butter is melted, add the apples, shallots, garlic, & mint. Sauté for 2 min. Add the couscous & olive oil & sauté for 1 min. Stir in the stock & bring to a boil, stirring for 2 min. Reduce the heat & cook for 1 min. Stir in the remaining butter & remove from the heat. Cover & allow to sit for 2 min. Uncover & fluff with a fork. Fold in the feta cheese. Season with S/P. Mound the couscous in the center of the platter. Lay the carved lamb over the couscous. Garnish with fresh rosemary & mint.

Prep Time: 15 min   **Cook Time:** 24 min
Nutritional Info: Calories 407.9 | Total Fat 8.0 g | Cholesterol 0.0 mg | Sodium 295.7 mg | Potassium 639.3 mg | Total Carbohydrate 51.6 g | Dietary Fiber 7.6 g | Sugars 1.9 g | Protein 36.9 g

ASPARAGUS PASTA
CATEGORIES: PASTA, ASPARAGUS, MUSTARD

Ingredients:
1 Cup Durum semolina
1/8 tsp Dry mustard/1/8 tsp Ground nutmeg
1/3 Cup Asparagus puree
2-3 tbsp. water if needed
1/3 Cup Asparagus puree
1 ¼ Cup Durum semolina
2 tbsp. Water if needed
1/8 tsp Dry mustard/1/8 tsp Nutmeg.

Instructions:
Fresh/canned asparagus may be used for the puree. Knead longer than usual. This seems to dry better dusted with flour & laid flat.

Prep Time: 0 min   **Cook Time:** 15 min
Nutritional Info: Calories 207.6 | Total Fat 7.0 g | Cholesterol 27.0 mg | Sodium 206.0 mg | Potassium 392.7

mg | Total Carbohydrate 25.4 g | Dietary Fiber 4.7 g | Sugars 1.0 g | Protein 14.3 g

BRIGHTON BEACH BAKE
CATEGORIES: PASTA

Ingredients:
1 tsp Sesame oil
2 medium-sized onions
3 cl Garlic
20g Brighton Beach Skewered Seaweed (aka Dried Arame)
3/4 lb. Mushrooms
2 medium-sized carrots
3 tsp vegetable stock
2 tsp Mirin
1 tsp Black Pepper
2 tsp Sea Salt
1.5 lb. Couscous
lots Water

Instructions:
Chop the onions & mince the garlic & fry in the sesame oil.
Soak the arame for about 15 min in boiling water. Then add
to the onion & garlic *without* the water used for soaking.
Add the finely chopped mushrooms & the grated carrots.
Mix the stock in some boiling hot water & add to the dish.

At the same time, add the leftover water from soaking the arame. Add the mirin & S/P to taste. It is probably best to have it slightly on the salty side as the saltiness will disappear when the couscous is added. Simmer the mixture covered for about 20 min. In a large mixing bowl add the couscous & the mixture together & any extra water required to cover. Leave for five min. Grease a large baking tray & line with baking parchment. Add the mixture to the baking tray & place in the oven covered with foil. Bake for about 20 min. Remove the foil & if the bake is still too wet continue for another 5--10 min. The top should be slightly browned, grill if necessary. We were originally going to add sesame seeds to this but forgot to as we were making it. Sesame seeds might be a good idea & would be especially useful if you wanted a dish without any added salt. You can also use a dried seaweed blend instead of salt.

Prep Time: 10 min
Cook Time: 24 min
Nutritional Info:

SPINACH PASTA
CATEGORIES: PASTA, SPINACH, MACHINE

Ingredients:
Hand:
2 Cup semolina flour durum
10 Oz pkg. chopped spinach cooked
Extruder:
2 ¾ Cup semolina flour durum   1 pkg. chopped spinach (10 Oz)

Instructions:
In this recipe you're supposed to drain the spinach, reserving any excess liquid & add as needed to form an edible dough. This recipe may be more challenging to roll out in a hand-crank machine.

Prep Time: 0 min   **Cook Time:** 20 min
Nutritional Info: Calories 37.1 | Total Fat 0.3 g |

Cholesterol 9.4 mg | Sodium 1.7 mg | Potassium 10.5 mg | Total | Carbohydrate 7.1 g | Dietary Fiber 0.0 g | Sugars 0.0 g | Protein 1.4 g

ALMOND TOPPED PEAR PIE
CATEGORIES: PIE, PEAR

Ingredients:
3 tbsp. Cornstarch
1/4 tsp Ginger Ground
1/8 tsp Salt
1/2 Cup Dark Corn Syrup
2 tbsp. Margarine
1 Unbaked 9" Pie Shell
1 tsp Lemon Juice
1/2 tsp Lemon Rind Grate
4 Pears pare thin-slice
Topping:
1 Cup Unbleached Flour
1/2 Cup Brown Sugar Firm Pack
1/4 tsp Ginger Ground
1/2 Cup Margarine
1/2 Cup Almonds Coarse Chop

Instructions:
Mix cornstarch, ginger & salt in a bowl. Add corn syrup, melted butter, lemon juice & lemon rind, stir till smooth. Add pears & toss till well coated with corn syrup mixture. Put the mixture in unbaked pie shell. Prepare Almond Topping & sprinkle over pears. Bake in a 400F oven 15 min then reduce heat to 350F. Bake an additional 30 min/till the topping & crust are golden browns. Cool on a wire rack.

ALMOND TOPPING: Combine the flour, brown sugar, & ginger in a bowl. Cut in the butter, using a pastry blender, till crumbly. Stir in the almonds.

Prep Time: 10 min   **Cook Time:** 50 min
Nutritional Info: Calories 176.9 | Total Fat 11.8 g | Cholesterol 41.4 mg | Sodium 10.1 mg | Potassium 185.6 mg | Total Carbohydrate 16.7 g | Dietary Fiber 3.3 g | Sugars 0.5 g | Protein 3.5 g

AMISH PEACH PIE
CATEGORIES: PIE, PEACH

Ingredients:
1/2 Cup Sugar
19" unbaked pie shell
1/4 tsp Salt
2 1/2 tbsp. Tapioca
4 Cup Peaches; peeled & sliced
Crumbs:
1/4 Cup Flour
2 1/2 tbsp. margarine melted
1/2 tsp Cinnamon
1/3 Cup Brown sugar

Instructions:
Mix gently, peaches, sugar, salt & tapioca. Let blend for 5 min before spooning into pie shell. Mix crumb ingredients well & sprinkle over pie shell. Bake at 425F for 45--50 min.

Prep Time: 0 min   **Cook Time:** 55 min
Nutritional Info: Calories 548.0 | Total Fat 35.6 g | Cholesterol 142.5 mg | Sodium 28.0 mg | Potassium 246.3

mg | Total Carbohydrate 62.3 g | Dietary Fiber 6.0 g | Sugars 26.8 g | Protein 7.3 g

BLACKBERRY PIE
CATEGORIES: PIE, BLACKBERRY

Ingredients:
1 Cup sugar
2 ½ tbsp. flour
1/4 tsp salt
4 cup fresh blackberries
1 egg yolk
3 tbsp. water
1 recipe plain pastry

Instructions:
Mix sugar, flour & salt. Wash blackberries & toss with flour mixture. Line pie pan with one half plain pastry recipe & fill with blackberry mixture. Top mixture with sec half of pastry recipe & press edges together. Prick/cut top to allow steam to escape. You can add shine to your finished pie by brushing the top with a mixture of 1 egg yolk & three tbsp. water before baking. Bake at 450F for 10 min, then reduce to 350F & bake for 25 more min. Remove when the crust is

brown & mixture is cooked through.

Prep Time: 10 min   **Cook Time:** 35 min
Nutritional Info: Calories 217.1 | Total Fat 7.0 g | Cholesterol 0.0 mg | Sodium 146.4 mg | Potassium 171.2 mg | Total Carbohydrate 34.9 g | Dietary Fiber 4.3 g | Sugars 7.6 g | Protein 2.4 g

CHEESE CUSTARD PIE
CATEGORIES: PIE, CHEESE

Ingredients:
3/4 lb. Cottage Cheese
3 Eggs
3/4 Cup Sugar
1 Heaping tbsp. Flour
1 1/4 Cup Milk
1 tsp Pure Vanilla Extract

Instructions:
Put cottage cheese through a sieve. Add sugar, flour, egg yolks, milk & vanilla extract. Mix well. Beat egg whites till stiff. Fold egg whites into the mixture. Pour into crust & bake for 3/4 hr. in a medium oven (350F).

Prep Time: 10 min   **Cook Time:** 15 min
Nutritional Info: Calories 150.9 | Total Fat 8.9 g | Cholesterol 111.1 mg | Sodium 158.5 mg | Potassium 48.8 mg | Total Carbohydrate 17.1 g | Dietary Fiber 0.2 g | Sugars 10.7 g | Protein 5.8 g

CRANBERRY PEAR PIE
CATEGORIES: PIE, PEAR

Ingredients:
5 medium pears
1 tsp ground cinnamon
1 Cup sugar
1 tbsp. margarine cut up
1/4 cup AP flour
1 tbsp. finely shredded orange peel
2 Cup cranberries
Pastry for a double-crust pie
Glazed Nut Topping
Sweetened whipped cream (optional)

Instructions:
Peel, core, & slice pears (should have 5 Cup). In a mixing bowl combine sugar, flour, orange peel, & cinnamon. Add pears & cranberries. Toss to coat. Set aside.
For pie shell:
Prepare double-crust pastry. Roll out half of the pastry; line a 9" pie plate with pastry. Fill the pastry-lined pie plate with

pear mixture. Dot filling with margarine. Trim bottom pastry to 1/2-inch beyond the edge of the plate. Roll out remaining pastry; cut into 1/2"-wide strips. Weave strips on top of filling to make a lattice. Press ends of strips into the rim of bottom crust. Fold bottom pastry over strips. Seal & crimp edge. Cover edge of pie with foil. Bake in a 375F oven for 25 min. Remove foil; bake for 25--30 min more/till crust is golden. Spoon Glazed Nut Topping evenly over warm pie. Cool pie on a wire rack before serving. Serve with sweetened whipped cream, if desired.

Glazed Nut Topping:

In a small saucepan combine 1/2 C chopped walnuts & 2 tbsp. Margarine. Cook & stir on medium heat till nuts are lightly browned. Stir in 3 tbsp. brown sugar. Heat & stir till sugar is dissolved. Stir in 1 tbsp. milk.

Prep Time: 40 min   **Cook Time:** 1 hour, 10 mins

Nutritional Info: Calories 255.0 | Total Fat 8.4 g | Cholesterol 20.3 mg | Sodium 141.9 mg | Potassium 182.0 mg | Total Carbohydrate 45.1 g | Dietary Fiber 3.2 g | Sugars 8.8 g | Protein 2.2 g

ACINI DI PEPE SALAD
CATEGORIES: SALAD, PASTA

Ingredients:
1 Cup White Sugar
20 Oz Crushed Pineapple
2 Eggs beat 7 Oz Mini Marshmallows
3 tbsp. AP Flour
15 Oz Mandarin Oranges
1 Cup Acini de Pepe Pasta
8 Oz container Cool Whip, thawed
1/2 tsp Salt
10 Oz Maraschino Cherries (optional)

Instructions:
Bring enough water to cook the pasta to a boil. Cook the pasta for 8--10 min/till al dente. Drain & set aside. In a medium saucepan, combine the liquid from the pineapple & oranges, sugar, eggs, salt & flour. Cook till the mixture is thick, stirring constantly. When thick, add in the pasta & refrigerate overnight. The next day, add in the pineapple, oranges, cool whip & marshmallows to taste. Mix well. Top with maraschino cherries if desired. Keep chilled till served.

Prep Time: 15 min   **Cook Time**: 30 min
Nutritional Info: Calories 229.1 | Total Fat 2.1 g | Cholesterol 21.3 mg | Sodium 12.9 mg | Potassium 70.3 mg | Total Carbohydrate 48.3 g | Dietary Fiber 1.7 g | Sugars 30.8 g | Protein 3.9 g

BLACK BEAN & BARLEY SALAD
CATEGORIES: SALAD, BEAN

Ingredients:
1-1/2 cup water
3/4 Cup frozen corn, thawed
1/2 cup pearled barley
1 cup black beans drained
1/2 avocado, chopped
2 tbsp. fresh cilantro, chopped
1/4 cup water
1/2 Cup green peas thawed if frozen
1 tbsp. lemon juice
3/4 cup peeled tomatoes, drained & chopped
1-1/2 tsp olive oil
1 scallion, white part only, finely chopped
1 cl Garlic, minced
1/4 lb. Pkg. salad

Instructions:
Bring water to a boil in a heavy pot. Add barley & reduce heat to low. Cover & simmer 35--40 min till the water has

evaporated & barley is tender. Remove from heat. Transfer barley to a cookie sheet. Spread barley out to cool briefly. While barley is cooking, combine next 7 ingredients & salt to taste in a bowl. Cover & refrigerate till barley is cooled. Combine remaining ingredients, except lettuce, in a jar with a tight-fitting lid. Shake vigorously till emulsified. Set aside. Transfer cooled barley to bean & vegetable mixture. Toss. Add dressing & toss again. Serve on a bed of lettuce.

Prep Time: 15 min   **Cook Time:** 50 min
Nutritional Info: Calories 335.5 | Total Fat 15.2 g | Cholesterol 0.0 mg | Sodium 592.5 mg | Potassium 405.8 mg | Total Carbohydrate 43.2 g | Dietary Fiber 10.5 g | Sugars 0.4 g | Protein 9.2 g

BLACK EYED PEA SALAD
CATEGORIES: SALAD, PEA, APPETIZER, GREEK

Ingredients:
3 cl Garlic minced
3 tbsp. Fresh ginger grated
Olive oil
2 Cup Black-eyed peas
Wine vinegar
3 tsp ground coriander
Salt
Hungarian paprika
1/2 Red pepper chopped OR cayenne to taste

Instructions:
Soak peas. Put in a pot with water to cover plus 1" & add coriander, garlic, ginger & red pepper. Cook for a little over 1 hr. till still a little chewy. While the peas are cooking, prepare the dressing by mixing oil, vinegar, salt & paprika. Use 2:1 oil-vinegar ratio & add seasonings according to

taste. Add to peas as soon as you remove them from the heat. Allow to cool to room temp & adjust seasoning then serve.

Prep Time: 10 min   **Cook Time:** 20 min
Nutritional Info: Calories 166.0 | Total Fat 5.3 g | Cholesterol 0.0 mg | Sodium 22.3 mg | Potassium 212.3 mg | Total Carbohydrate 28.6 g | Dietary Fiber 6.7 g | Sugars 7.1 g | Protein 4.2 g

CHERRY DELIGHT SALAD
CATEGORIES: SALAD, CHERRY

Ingredients:
1 Cup cherry pie filling
1 medium Cup crushed pineapple
1 Cup Eagle Brand milk
1 large Cup chunk pineapple drained
1 large carton Cool Whip

Instructions:
Mix. Fold in Cool Whip. Refrigerate.

Prep Time: 20 min   **Cook Time:** 5 min
Nutritional Info: Calories 400.6 | Total Fat 12.3 g | Cholesterol 14.0 mg | Sodium 363.2 mg | Potassium 134.5 mg | Total Carbohydrate 68.6 g | Dietary Fiber 1.6 g | Sugars 33.3 g | Protein 6.1 g

CHINESE CHICKEN SALAD
CATEGORIES: SALAD, CHICKEN, CHINESE

Ingredients:
8 Oz Fresh bean sprouts
1 Plain roasted chicken about 2 1/2 lb.
2 medium Cucumbers
1 Carrots (or double amount)
2 tsp Sesame oil
2 tbsp. Chinese white rice vinegar (cider vinegar)
3 tbsp. Light soy sauce
1 ½ tbsp. Finely chopped garlic
1 tsp Salt
3 tbsp. Sesame paste (or peanut butter)
2 tsp Sugar
2 tbsp. Finely chopped scallions
2/3 cup Chicken stock
1 tbsp. Rice wine/dry sherry

Instructions:
Trim the bean sprouts at both ends. Peel the cucumber split it in half lengthwise & remove the seeds with a tsp. Finely

shred the cucumber into 3" lengths. Peel & finely shred the carrots into 3-in lengths. Set the vegetables aside. Take all the meat off the cooked chicken & shred it into fine strips using a sharp knife/cleaver. Arrange the chicken strips on a platter & surround them with the bean sprouts, cucumbers & carrots. Combine all the ingredients for the dressing & mix them thoroughly. (an electric blender is useful for this, but you could use a screw-top jar & shake everything in it well.) Pour the dressing all over the chicken & vegetables & mix well.

Prep Time: 10 min   **Cook Time:** 15 min
Nutritional Info: Calories 150.0 | Total Fat 3.0 g | Cholesterol 0.0 mg | Sodium 448.0 mg | Potassium 0.0 mg | Total Carbohydrate 11.0 g | Dietary Fiber 3.0 g | Sugars 0.0 g | Protein 20.0 g

CONGEALED SALAD
CATEGORIES: SALAD, CARROT

Ingredients:
Dissolve:
1 pkg. lime Jell-O in
1 cup boiling water
Add:
1 small cup crushed pineapple
1/2 cup mayonnaise
1 small cup evaporated milk
1 carton cottage cheese (1 lb.)
1/2 cup chopped nuts

Instructions:
Mix & place in the refrigerator to congeal.

Prep Time: 15 min   **Cook Time:** 2 min
Nutritional Info: Calories 161.9 | Total Fat 10.1 g | Cholesterol 6.3 mg | Sodium 73.4 mg | Potassium 197.8 mg | Total Carbohydrate 15.1 g | Dietary Fiber 1.9 g | Sugars 2.9 g | Protein 3.3 g

APPLE HARVEST OATMEAL
CATEGORIES: VEGETABLE, SQUASH

Ingredients:
1 ½ cup milk
1/2 tsp cinnamon
1 ½ Cup water
1 ½ Cup oats, quick
2 tbsp. Raisins 2 tbsp. brown sugar
1 Cup or more chopped peeled apples

Instructions:
In a saucepan, bring milk & water to boil. Stir in remaining ingredients & cook till thick. Cover & let stand a few mins. Serve.

Prep Time: 15 min **Cook Time:** 5 min
Nutritional Info: Calories 130 | Total Fat 1.5g | Cholesterol 0mg | Sodium 170mg | Total Carbohydrate 27g | Dietary Fiber 3g | Sugars 12g | Protein 3g

BATTER CRISP ONION RINGS
CATEGORIES: VEGETABLE, ONION, EGG, FLOUR

Ingredients:
3 large sweet onions, sliced into 1/4" & separated into rings
1 ½ tsp baking powder
1 cup flour
1/2 tsp salt
1 egg
2/3 cup water
1/2 tbsp. lemon juice
1 tbsp. melted butter
Oil for frying

Instructions:
Soak the onion rings in ice water for at least 1/2 hr. Pat the onion rings dry with paper towels. Sift together the baking powder, flour & salt. Combine the egg, water, & lemon juice & beat till frothy. Stir this into the dry ingredients just till blended. Add butter. Dip onion rings into batter, a few at a time. Drop into 375F oil. Fry 2 min on each side, turning

once. Drain on absorbent paper. Keep hot in slow oven (325F) till all are cooked. Don't crowd them in the fryer.

Prep Time: 10 min   **Cook Time:** 20 min
Nutritional Info: Calories 170.2 | Total Fat 6.1 g | Cholesterol 26.8 mg | Sodium 411.9 mg | Potassium 44.3 mg | Total Carbohydrate 24.9 g | Dietary Fiber 0.5 g | Sugars 2.2 g | Protein 4.5 g

BORANI ESFANAA

CATEGORIES: **VEGETABLE,**   **SPINACH,**
YOGURT, ONION

Ingredients:
1 Cup yogurt
2 onions, thinly sliced
cooking oil
2 lb. fresh spinach
S/P
4 cl of garlic, finely chopped (optional)

Instructions:
Wash spinach & cut into small pieces. Fry onions & garlic in oil till slightly golden. Add spinach & fry together over medium heat till cooked. Let it cool down completely in the refrigerator. Add S/P to yogurt to taste & beat well till the yogurt is a free-flowing liquid. Add spinach to yogurt & mix well. The mix should be thick & homogeneous. This delicious side-dish is now ready to serve.

Prep Time: 10 min   **Cook Time:** 15 min
Nutritional Info: Calories 224.0 | Total Fat 20.9 g |

Cholesterol 1.8 mg | Sodium 169.6 mg | Potassium 257.4 mg | Total Carbohydrate 8.1 g | Dietary Fiber 2.2 g | Sugars 2.2 g | Protein 2.6 g

CAULIFLOWER CHERRY LONGHORN
CATEGORIES: VEGETABLE, CAULIFLOWER, CHERRY

Ingredients:
4 sticks celery, sliced
1 ½ Cup ripe red cherries, pitted
1 red onion, finely chopped
1 cup avocado, peeled, destoned & diced
2 Cup whole egg mayonnaise
Red lettuce leaves to serve
3 tsp dried paprika
1/2 Cup Longhorn cheese, grated
1 1/2 Cup raw cauliflower florets, washed in saltwater

Instructions:
Combine cauliflower, cherries, celery, red onion & avocado in a salad bowl. Mix well & chill till needed. Using a food processor, blend mayonnaise, dried paprika & Longhorn cheese till smooth. Pour dressing over salad & mix well till well coated. Serve chilled on a bed of red lettuce with crusty

bread as an accompaniment to fish, meat/poultry.

Prep Time: 5 min   **Cook Time:** 15 min
Nutritional Info: Calories 300 | Total Carbs 19 g | Dietary
Fiber 6 g | Sugar 6 g | Total Fat 19 g | Protein 15 g |
Sodium 1070 mg | Potassium 0 mg | Cholesterol 50 mg

CREAMY PARSNIP MASH
CATEGORIES: PARSNIP, CREAM

Ingredients:
2 1/2 lb. small parsnips, peeled & quartere
3 chicken bouillon cubes
1 tbsp. fresh lemon juice
4 tbsp. butter, melted
1/2 cup heavy cream, warmed
S/P to taste
2 tbsp. snipped fresh chives

Instructions:
Place the parsnips in a saucepan with water to cover. Add the bouillon & lemon juice. Simmer for 20 min/till very tender drain. Mash, adding the butter & cream. Season with S/P. Serve immediately, garnished with snipped chives.

Prep Time: 10 min   **Cook Time:** 12 min
Nutritional Info: Calories 138.9 | Total Fat 4.0 g | Cholesterol 0.3 mg | Sodium 727.2 mg | Potassium 674.4

mg | Total Carbohydrate 25.3 g | Dietary Fiber 6.1 g | Sugars 9.5 g | Protein 2.7 g

EGGPLANT/SWISS CHEESE CASSEROLE

CATEGORIES: VEGETABLE, EGGPLANT, CHEESE

Ingredients:

1/2 cup Onion, chopped 2 tbsp. Dried Parsley Flakes
1 tbsp. Vegetable Oil
1/2 tsp Salt
6 Oz can Tomato Paste
1 large Eggplant or- Zucchini
1 ¾ Cup Water
1 lb. Swiss Cheese, sliced
2 tsp Dried Oregano
1 ½ Cup Dry Bread Cubes
1/4 Cup Parsley Leaves, freshly
1 Cup Parmesan Cheese, grated chopped or

Instructions:

Sauté the onion in the oil in a saucepan till the onion is tender. Add the tomato paste, water, oregano, parsley & salt. Simmer over low heat for 10 min. Cut the eggplant (or zucchini) into 1/4-inch-thick slices. Arrange one layer of eggplant slices in the bottom of a lightly-oiled 9-13" baking pan. Pour on about 1/3 Cup of the tomato sauce. Top with the Swiss cheese slices. Add another layer of eggplant slices & pour on about 1/2 Cup of the tomato sauce. Combine the rest of the sauce with the bread cubes and spoon over the eggplant. Sprinkle on the Parmesan Cheese. Bake in a 325F oven for about 25 min.

Prep Time: 15 min   **Cook Time:** 45 min
Nutritional Info: Calories 385 | Total Fat 26g | Cholesterol 72mg | Sodium 497mg | Total Carbohydrates 17g | Protein 4g

THINK A COMPLETE MEAL

Due to the fast-food era of today, kids are more prone to eat junk than healthy foods. It is the utmost duty of parents to make sure that kids eat a complete healthy meal. Your kids should eat a meal which consists of three basic food groups. This should include carbohydrate-rich foods which are the primary source of energy. There should be protein-rich foods and fruits and vegetables.

The reason why a complete meal must have the three different basic food groups is that the functions of a body do not only rely on what it can get from one type of food group. It needs all the benefits it can get from each of these food groups.

The carbohydrate-rich foods such as grains, cereals, and wheat provide the body the energy it needs to be able to do the tasks required for the day. This is the reason why kids need to eat breakfast before going to school, or else they won't have the energy to last them until the afternoon. Without a supply of carbohydrates, a kid's body would become weak and tired and would have a hard time coping up with the demands of school activities. And the function of a brain would be affected as well.

Kids need protein-rich foods such as meat and milk because these foods assist in building muscles. Not only that, tissues are restored and replaced due to protein. Proteins also maintain the immune system. When your kid is physically active like when he's involved in sports activities, he needs more protein intake.

Fruits and vegetables should not be missed out in your kid's meal. These are sources of vitamins and minerals which strengthen the immune system such as Vitamin C. Your kid's eyes need Vitamin A that comes from fruits and vegetables as well. So always remember that when you prepare your kid's meals, make sure that each type of basic food groups would be present. When you comply with this, you have now prepared a complete healthy meal for your kid.

FROM THE AUTHOR

What Did You Think of This Book?

First of all, thank you for purchasing this book. I know you could have picked any number of books to read, but you chose this book, and for that, I am incredibly grateful. I hope that it added value and quality to your everyday life. If so, it would be nice if you could share this book with your friends and family by posting to Facebook and Twitter.

If you enjoyed this book and found some benefit in reading this, I'd like to hear from you and hope that you could take some time to post a review on Amazon. Your feedback and support will help me to greatly improve my writing craft for future projects and make this book even better.

You can follow this link to see more of my books now.

I want you to know that your review is very important and so if you'd like to leave a review, all you have to do is click on the book link and scroll down. I wish you all the best in your future success!

Made in the USA
Middletown, DE
03 February 2023